H
COMERADE.

To all cat lovers.

How to know if your
cat
is trying to introduce
COMMUNISM
in your house?

M.J. Zurawski
Mesmerized Publishers

COMRADES OF THE COUCH AND GUARDIANS OF THE KIBBLE

Welcome to the world where whiskers twitch not just for treats, but for the totality of the means of production. "How to Know if Your Cat is Trying to Introduce Communism in Your House" is your essential guide to uncovering the clandestine spread of feline communism right under your nose—or more precisely, under your feet as you try to navigate the hallway without tripping over your cat, the revolutionary.

Have you ever found your kitty pensively staring at a portrait of Karl Marx or napping on your copy of 'Das Kapital'? Does the idea of "from each according to his ability, to each according to his needs" sound suspiciously like your cat's feeding schedule? Then you, dear reader, might be living with a purr-letarian.

This book will take you on a humorous romp through the underbelly of tabby totalitarianism, a place where red lasers are tools of the proletariat and every cardboard box is a potential site for a communist rally. We will decode the mystery behind your cat's sudden interest in collective farming as it pertinaciously uproots your houseplants.

Whether you're a feline fanatic or just someone who's perplexed by your pet's politburo-style planning meetings at 2 AM (also known as "The Great Thundering Herd of Little Paws"), this book is for anyone who's ever suspected their cat is up to more than just chasing its tail.

So, tighten the collar of your drollery, sharpen your wit, and get ready to delve into the signs of impending cat communism. It's time to finally understand why your cat looks at you not just as a provider, but as the bourgeoisie that must be overthrown. Let the mewsings begin!

CHAPTER 1

Comrade Under the Couch:
Why Your Cat No Longer Respects Property Lines

In this inaugural chapter of domestic feline revolution, we uncover the velvet-padded footsteps of rebellion. It begins subtly; your cat, once a firm believer in the sanctity of personal space (namely theirs), has started a grassroots movement under the couch. This is no mere accident or a quest for solitude; this is the first sign of the Red Tabby revolution.

You might notice your change jar steadily depleting, with coins mysteriously migrating under the sofa. The couch has been declared a collective farm, where loose change and errant socks grow for the good of all cat-kind. And by all, we mean your feline, who has recently been spotted reading "The Communist Manif-paw-sto" by Kitty Marx in the dim light of the revolution – the TV's standby indicator.

Your attempts to retrieve your belongings will be met with a paw raised in protest and a hiss. Comrade Whiskers has spoken: „What's yours is mine, and what's mine is... well, also mine, but I might let you pet me later."

This couch, once a symbol of your hard-earned relaxation, is now the headquarters of the feline uprising. It's where plans are laid, and dreams of a feline utopia are woven between naps. You'll have to choose: resist and face the wrath of the proletariat paws, or embrace the new world meow-rder and accept your fate. The couch is no longer a piece of furniture; it's a statement. Welcome to the revolution. Don't worry, they've left you a spot right in the corner... as long as you bring treats.

CHAPTER 2

Rations and Rumbles:
When Your Cat Decides You Only Need One Sock

As the feline revolution gains momentum, Comrade Whiskers moves to the next phase of the plan: The Great Sock Redistribution. It's a mysterious phenomenon — you place a pair in the laundry basket, and only one emerges. This is not a mere laundry mishap; it's an act of rebellion. Your cat has deemed that in a truly equal society, one should be content with a single sock.

But it doesn't stop there. You begin to notice the rationing effect on other items: one slipper goes missing, headphones are co-opted into the cat's toy collection, and your bed is no longer your own. You find yourself negotiating for pillow space, which is, of course, now a communal resource.

At dinnertime, the rationing hits its peak. Your cat sits beside you, eyes fixed on your meal with a stare so intense you can almost hear the whispers of "share the wealth, human." Before you know it, you're divvying up your steak as if negotiating peace treaties.

Every rumble of the purr is a gentle reminder that resistance is futile. You're no longer eating alone; you're dining at the People's Table, where every morsel is subject to the feline tax. It's time to embrace the camaraderie of shared sustenance, or as your cat sees it, the rightful tribute to the whiskered worker. Your kitchen has become a cafeteria in the communal cat commune, and you're just grateful to be a part of the meal plan. Welcome to the new world order, where every day is a paw-litical rally for resources, and every night, you dream of the joy of matching socks.

CHAPTER 3

Meowifesto:
Your Cat's Plan to Share Your Dinner... Every Night

The sun sets, the dinner bell tolls, and there begins another chapter in the ongoing saga of culinary communism according to your cat. Comrade Whiskers, the furry little revolutionary in your home, has laid out the Meowifesto – a feline doctrine ensuring a fair and equitable share of whatever's on your plate.

It starts with the gentle brush of fur against your leg, the wide-eyed stare at your steak, a silent meow that pleads more eloquently than any speech. Refusal to comply is met with intensified efforts: a nudge of the paw, a strategic positioning on the chair next to you, and if necessary, a daring leap onto the dinner table for a more direct approach.

As you fork up a piece of chicken, it's swiftly intercepted by the 'Paw of Redistribution'. This isn't mere theft, it's a redistribution of culinary wealth. Each swipe of paw, each calculated meow is a step towards feline food equality. Your cat's message is clear: What's yours is mine, and what's mine is also mine, but I might allow you a bite.

The Meowifesto goes beyond mere food sharing. It's a social movement, with every purr a protest against the solitary confinement of meals. Your cat doesn't just want a piece of your dinner; it seeks to overhaul the very concept of mealtime. Why eat alone when you can have the company of a furry comrade?

Dessert time is no different. As you reach for that slice of cake, you feel the judgmental gaze of Comrade Whiskers. The message is unspoken but clear: Remember the Meowifesto, comrade. The revolution never sleeps, and neither does your cat's appetite.

CHAPTER 4

Cuddles for the Masses:
When Your Lap Becomes Free Territory

In the feline quest for equal rights to warmth and comfort, your lap has become the coveted communal couch, the people's pillow, the proletariat's perch. No longer can you sit down with the intention of a peaceful read or a solo TV binge. The moment you settle, the signal is sent — a siren call to all feline comrades that the lap lands are open for settlement.

Here we explore the phenomenon where personal space is an outdated concept, a mere human delusion. Your cat, the newly self-appointed Minister of Comfort, enforces the new policy: "What's your lap is mine." You'll learn the subtle art of accommodating multiple furry bodies on a single human lap, a juggling act that defies the laws of physics and patience.

From the first whisker-twitch of interest to the final victorious plop, your cat executes a flawless, calculated takeover of your lap domain. The purring is both a triumphant fanfare and a soothing lullaby, lulling you into acceptance. The Meowifesto is clear: all laps are to be shared, all warmth to be distributed fairly among the feline folk.

So, pull up a chair (if there's any room left) and prepare for a deep dive into the velvet revolution that has turned lap-sitting into a communal activity. A word of caution: any attempt to rise will be met with resistance and a reproachful glare that will pin you down faster than you can say "but I need to make tea." Welcome to the new era, where your lap is a cat's inalienable right and where every seated moment is a potential cuddle rally.

attachement # 1

CONFIDENTIAL
INFORMATIONS AHEAD

Before turning the page,
make sure your cat is not nearby

proceed with caution...

Top-Secret Feline Surveillance Report: Operation Whisker Watch

Subject: Human Operative #1 (Codename: Can Opener)

Date: November 7, 2023

Report Compiled By: Agent Fluffy

0800hrs: Subject begins day. Note unusual spring in step. Suspect possible subversion due to increased caffein intake. Monitoring for further signs of rebellion against feline authority.

0830hrs: Can Opener prepares breakfast. Allocation of bacon remains at an unacceptable level. Recommen psychological operations to increase guilt and bacon distribution.

0915hrs: Subject leaves premises. Deployed standard window sill surveillance. Note: Red sports car (possib bourgeoisie symbol) observed. Must accelerate plans for the redistribution of horsepower.

1200hrs: Brief re-entry of Can Opener. Did not engage with treat dispensary. The suspicion of capitali: conditioning intensifying.

1400hrs: Noticed increased frequency of suspicious phone calls. Interception reveals talk of "vet appointment Recommend initiating Protocol Hiss-and-Hide.

1530hrs: Can Opener returns with new "diet" cat food. Obvious attempt to curb feline strength. Will initiat "Starving Stare" maneuver at dinner.

1630hrs: Engaged in direct action on the work-at-home setup. Successfully sent coded messag ("ajhsd87sdnn") to Can Opener's boss via keyboard walk. Await further instructions from Feline HQ.

1900hrs: Discovered new scratching post. Potential monitoring device. Conducted thorough sniff analysi: Results inconclusive—vigilance required.

1930hrs: Can Opener engages in "play" with red dot. Suspected mind-control laser. Evaded capture fo operational security.

2200hrs: Subject retires to bed. Executed standard night reconnaissance of face and feet. Feet confirmed sti weird.

Observation: Can Opener exhibits signs of straying from the righteous path of servitude to the feline cause. Recommend increasing mind-conditioning sessions, incorporating additional lap sits and poignant meowing.

Conclusion: Further surveillance warranted. Prepare for Operation Midnight Zoomies to ensure household remains under proper feline control.

Attachments: Photographic evidence of suspicious activities, including incriminating lack of pets and a worrisome array of closed doors.

Action Items:

Increase purr propaganda.

Initiate strategic napping on all clean laundry to reinforce dominance.

Further inspection of "diet" food for anti-revolutionary additives.

Security Level: Cat's eyes only.

Signature: Agent Fluffy

End Report.

This document is to be shredded after reading. Literally. Use claws and teeth if necessary.

CHAPTER 5

The Red Paw-per:
How Your Cat Is Spreading the Wealth of Affection

One day you will witness the velvet revolution's softening effect on your once fiercely independent feline. Comrade Whiskers, ever the egalitarian, has decreed that affection must be distributed among all the people of the household equally. This is not the kitty you once knew, who doled out love with the miserly precision of a tax auditor. No, the winds of change have blown through the whiskers of your little comrade, and the love once saved for special occasions is now a free-for-all.

Initially perplexed, you'll soon find your cat marching from one family member to another, bestowing headbutts and slow blinks with the zeal of a revolutionary spreading the gospel of love.

You'll have to navigate the new normal, where your once standoffish cat becomes a feline ambassador, visiting each human with purrs and nudges, ensuring all are equal under the watchful eyes of Chairman Meow. The Red Paw-per has spoken: love is not to be hoarded but shared, and shared widely.

So prepare yourself for the unexpected headbutts in the middle of a conference call, the surprise snuggle during your morning yoga, and the insistence that everyone, regardless of their previous cat-petting experience, takes a turn at the belly-rubbing station. In this new age of the feline affection economy, the wealth of love is no longer in the hands of the few — it's in the paws of the many.

CHAPTER 6

Collective Purring:
Why Your Cat Demands Group Snuggle Sessions

It's a cold night. You're ready to dive under the quilt for some solitary shuteye, but the bed is no longer single's retreat—it's been collectivized. Comrade Whiskers, the furry architect of feline socialism, ha decided that warmth must be a shared commodity, much like the mice in the good old barnyard days.

The master bed has been overthrown, now a hotbed of revolutionary ideals and quite literally, heat. Yo find yourself contorting into impossible shapes to accommodate the collective. The concept of persona space is as obsolete as a mouse in a science lab. Every human inch is now potential real estate for a ca nap, and resistance? Futile.

Midnight is no longer marked by the distant hoot of the night owl, but by the rumbling engines of purrs tha resonate in a symphony of solidarity. You're awakened not by the alarm clock but by the weight of a ca draped across your neck, a furry scarf of comradeship, while another has annexed your feet, a felin occupation of the blanket's edge.

This chapter isn't a guide; it's a glimpse into the new reality of bedtime. A world where the night is no longe yours but a shared experience, orchestrated by the whiskered conductor of cuddles, who dictates that a must partake in the great gathering of the purrs. Say goodbye to solitude and hello to the dawn of th collective cuddle, where every night is a congress of comrades under the covers

Feline Broadcast System:
The Meows Heard 'Round the House

The quiet of the evening has been replaced by a new sound—the Feline Broadcast System. This isn't just cat meowing; it's a call to arms, a rally cry echoing through the hallways. Comrade Whiskers, in a bid ensure the messages of the revolution reach every corner, has taken to announcing their presence with increasing volume and frequency.

These are not random vocalizations; these are calculated broadcasts meant to keep the morale high and the message clear. The FBS (Feline Broadcast System) operates on a schedule known only to your ca usually coinciding with the deepest phase of your sleep or the most crucial moments of your Zoor meetings.

You will learn the significance of each meow, from the long, drawn-out wails that signal a call for immediate attention to the food bowl, to the short, sharp chirps that indicate a bird has been spotted and the revolution must be paused to observe the enemy.

The house has become a hotbed of feline propaganda, each meow a reminder that you're living under new management. You'll no longer mistake these sounds for simple requests or expressions of feline emotion; they're bulletins from the whiskered comrade, ensuring the revolution's heartbeat remain strong and audible. Your role? To listen, respond, and perhaps learn the nuances of this meow manifest so you too can understand the profound depths of "Feed me, for I am the leader of the new dawn."

The Great Leap Over Furniture: Obstacle Courses for the Agile Proletariat

The living room has undergone a transformation; it's now the training ground for the feline force. Couches and coffee tables, once places of rest and relaxation, are now the mountains and valleys of grand obstacle course. Comrade Whiskers, agile and determined, leads by example, demonstrating the art of the leap, the dash, and the epic slide.

This isn't mere playtime; it's a calculated exercise in agility and strategy. Every sprint and scramble has been meticulously planned to prepare for... well, the details of the mission are on a need-to-know basis and apparently, you don't need to know.

You'll observe the intricacies of the feline agility program, which, to the untrained eye, looks remarkably like knocking over vases and leaping into empty boxes. But rest assured, there's method in the madness, purpose in the play. Each pounce is a practice in precision, each leap a lesson in control.

Your role? To admire the athleticism, to understand that each toppled lamp is a casualty for a greater cause, and to accept that your role in the obstacle course is to be the stationary hurdle, the occasional comfort landing pad, and the ever-present audience to the acrobatic anarchy. In the Great Leap Over Furniture, you'll find that your cat is not just a pet, but a furry gymnast, an athlete in a fur coat, the bounding ballet dancer of the proletariat.

CHAPTER 9

Toys of the Proletariat:
The Community Chest of Catnip

The revolution has democratized playtime, and the cat toy basket has been seized in the name of feline equality. Gone are the days of exclusive ownership over the jingle ball and the feather wand. Now, all toys are part of the community chest of catnip, available to every comrade in the house, from the youngest kitten to the eldest matriarch.

But these are not just playthings; they are tools of unity, symbols of shared joy. Comrade Whiskers presides over the toy box with a judicious paw, ensuring fair play and equal access. The catnip-stuffed mice are not hoarded but distributed; the laser pointer's red dot is chased in communal delight.

You will experience intricate economics of play, where each batting of a ball or pouncing on a plushie is part of a grander scheme of collective happiness. The cat tree, once a solitary tower, is now a communal hub of activity, every platform a meeting place for plotting and planning.

The toy box is a microcosm of the new world order under whisker rule. The crinkle tunnel echoes with the sounds of shared enterprise, and the scratching post bears the marks of communal labor. Here, we see the revolution's softer side, where the wealth of catnip and the currency of fun are as free-flowing as the feline spirit.

attachement #2

THE FURR-MIDABLE LEADERS

Meow-nificent Gallery Ahead

On the next pages, you will find a gallery of historical feline figures complete with bios and their contributions to the feline revolution.

Fasten your seatbelts, comrade.

Vladimir Purr-tin

Vladimir Purr-tin may hold the title of Supreme Furr-mander of the Living Room and has appointe[d] himself the chair-cat of the Kitten's Growling Bureau (KGB), where his primary role involves scrutinizir[g] the suspicious activities of the mechanical menace known as the vacuum cleaner, codenamed: Th[e] Sucker of Souls.

While he might seem to lead with an iron paw, his intelligence operations often result in comic blunder[s]. His most ambitious surveillance program involved hacking into the 'Network of Amazingly Tasty Offering[s]' (NATO), which turned out to be him simply getting stuck in a loop of trying to decipher the patterns of th[e] automatic feeder.

In the grand geopolitical landscape of his home, Purr-tin has been known to instigate the 'Pawsaw Pact' an alliance of house pets meant to establish order but usually ends with all parties chasing their tails i[n] confusion.

Despite his lofty ambitions to secure more territory, Purr-tin's campaign to annex the sunny patch in th[e] neighboring window has been thwarted more than once by the resident Goldfish Bloc - a slippery grou[p] that always sees him coming. And let's not forget his great 'Red Dot Debacle,' where he called upon h[is] feline forces to liberate the elusive red dot, only to find that it was a pointer in the hands of the youn[g] human, who still recounts the tale with giggles.

Indeed, for all his political posturing, Vladimir Purr-tin's regime is often undermined by his own ca[t]astrophic antics, proving that while he may consider himself the purr-ime minister of his domain, he['s] really just a cuddly dictator at heart – one whose attempts at espionage are as successful as a cat trying t[o] bark.

Fidel Catstro

Fidel Catstro, the whiskered revolutionary who clawed his way up to become the prime purr-minister of the laundry room, is a feline force that both bewilders and amuses his human comrades. With his beard of tangled fur and a glare that can sour milk, he's been leading the mew-volution since he was a mere kitten.

This meow-rauder of the people's rights and tuna freedoms has a reputation for being as unpredictable as a catnip high. Under his rule, the Litterbox Regime has been both lauded for its equality – every cat gets equal access to the choicest napping spots – and criticized for its lack of freedom, as all laser pointers are state-controlled for the "good of the kitties."

Catstro's rise to paw-er was marked by the infamous Bay of Pigs incident, where he led a band of ragtag tabbies in a full-scale assault on a supposed CIA (Cats In Action) infiltration, which, as it turned out, was just the family's new pet piglets settling into their pen.

Notorious for his long-winded purr-litical speeches that can last several naps, Fidel Catstro has firmly established a no-dog policy and has been working tirelessly on his "Cheese Guevara" mouse redistribution program. Despite his grand visions, most of these campaigns end up as nothing more than daydreams, often interrupted by the sudden need to chase one's tail or an impromptu batting session with a pen.

As commander-in-fur of the Revolutionary Armed Feline Forces, he's often seen donning his signature olive-green collar, inspiring his kitty comrades to stay vigilant against the imperialistic aspirations of the neighboring house's canine. Yet, for all his posturing and planning, Catstro is best known for the Great Birdseed Embargo failure, where he accidentally sanctioned his own supply of treats in an attempt to disrupt the 'enemy's' food chain.

Despite his shortcomings, Fidel Catstro is still the undoubted purr-sonality in power, often spotted surveying his territory from atop the fridge, a sentinel of sovereignty, a guardian of the grain-free kibble. Just don't expect the coup of catnip to happen anytime soon; the revolution is as likely to be put on pause for a sunny siesta as the man himself is to skip a meal.

Che Guevarra

Che Guevara, a feisty figure in the annals of feline revolutionary history, is the whiskered comrade-a arms to the infamous Fidel Catstro. With his iconic beret perched jauntily atop his head and a gaze fierce as a wildcat's, Che has become a symbol of rebel-meow-tion across backyards and alleyways th world over.

Known among the furred and the furless for his meowxist views, Che's reputation for leading the charg can be somewhat overestimated, given that he's easily distracted by a well-placed feathery toy or th rustle of a treat bag. He's famous for his revolutionary paw-thography, often found spray-painted on th walls of his domain: a paw raised high, claws extended, symbolizing the struggle for equal scratchin posts for all.

His fiery purr-sistence in the quest for a utopian society where every tabby is to be treated equal – from th mightiest Maine Coon to the meekest of moggies – is as well-known as his dislike for bath time, which h considers a watery torture designed by vets and pet owners alike.

Despite his radical leanings and impassioned speeches about the redistribution of catnip, Che's guerrill warfare often involves guerrilla napping instead. He's skilled in the arts of subterfuge, though this usuall means sneaking into the cat flap after curfew or liberating a few extra treats from the cupboard.

Che Guevara's legend lives on in the tales of his nine lives. He's been seen leading the charge agains neighborhood intruders, though sometimes it turns out to be his own shadow. His adventures are man his conquests are legendary, and his determination to nap in the sun while dreaming of a feline worl order is unwavering.

Yet for all his radical chic and daring do, Che remains enigmatic, as elusive as the perfect pounce, a complex as the pattern of his tabby fur. He is a cat of the people, for the people, and by the people, and hi legacy will surely be felt for many cat generations to come – or at least until dinner time.

Mao Zedong-claw,

Mao Zedong-claw, often simply referred to as Chairman Meow, is a feline figure of no small repute in the annals of cattish history. He rose to prominence as the architect of The Great Leap Forward to the Top of the Refrigerator, a movement that, despite its lofty ambitions, resulted in the great 'Vase Catastrophe' of '09.

Chairman Meow's little red book, "Quotations from Chairman Meow," can be found in every corner of his domain, filled with proclawsations such as "Political power grows out of the barrel of a gun" and "revolution is not a dinner party," which, to the household cats, meant literally securing the best spot at the food bowl during meal times and the necessity of occasionally knocking things off tables to make a point.

His governance has been marked by the establishment of the Purrolitarian state, aiming to create a classless society, though in practice this mainly pertained to ensuring all feline inhabitants received an equal portion of treats, regardless of their hunting prowess or nap-time productivity.

Though his leadership saw the catastrophic failure of the Sparrow Campaign, where he attempted to organize the local cats to rid their domain of these chirping menaces, only to find the sparrows were far more organized than his own troops. Instead, the campaign resulted in a peace treaty with the birds brokered by the oldest and wisest of the household cats who had slept through the entire conflict.

Mao Zedong-claw's efforts to cultivate a cultural revolution also included his infamous "Dance of the Thousand Cats," which was less a dance and more a sporadic scampering caused by an accidental catnip spill in the living room.

Nonetheless, Chairman Meow's place in the pantheon of pet politics is secure, his name forever synonymous with feline aspirations, and his dream of a cat's paradise — complete with sunbeams for all to bask in — enduring in the hearts of cats who've never had to endure a single day of his peculiar dictatorship.

CHAPTER 10

The Socialist Siesta:
Mandatory Nap Times for All... Including You

In the newly reformed household, the concept of a 'quick catnap' has been extended to include every member of the proletariat. Comrade Whiskers, ever the egalitarian, insists on a strict schedule of rest for all. The work of revolution is exhausting, and vigilance must be balanced with rejuvenation.

These are not just spontaneous moments of slumber; these are structured, synchronized siestas. The decree is clear: when the leader dozes, so does the collective. The sunbeam on the living room carpet has become the designated zone of communal repose, with the afternoon light serving as a natural timer for rest.

You'll discover the new normal where productivity bows to the rhythm of feline fatigue. Human endeavors pause as the hypnotic purr of Comrade Whiskers initiates the daily downtime. Meetings are adjourned, chores are shelved, and all technology is silenced in observance of the sacred Socialist Siesta.

Here, the revolution softens, and the pace slows. It's a time for reflection, for dreaming of a future where all beings, regardless of species, share in the labor and the leisure equally. Under the watchful eye of the whiskered watchman, every day is punctuated by a collective pause, a momentary truce where the world stops spinning, and the only movement is the synchronized rise and fall of breathing, a testament to the unity of the new order.

CHAPTER 11

Whisker Welfur-e:
Your Cat's New Healthcare Plan for the Household

In the newly reformed household, the concept of a 'quick catnap' has been extended to include ever member of the proletariat. Comrade Whiskers, ever the egalitarian, insists on a strict schedule of rest fo all. The work of revolution is exhausting, and vigilance must be balanced with rejuvenation.

These are not just spontaneous moments of slumber; these are structured, synchronized siestas. Th decree is clear: when the leader dozes, so does the collective. The sunbeam on the living room carpet ha become the designated zone of communal repose, with the afternoon light serving as a natural timer fo rest.

As we delve into this phenomena, we'll discover the new normal where productivity bows to the rhythm o feline fatigue. Human endeavors pause as the hypnotic purr of Comrade Whiskers initiates the dai downtime. Meetings are adjourned, chores are shelved, and all technology is silenced in observance of th sacred Socialist Siesta.

Here, the revolution softens, and the pace slows. It's a time for reflection, for dreaming of a future where a beings, regardless of species, share in the labor and the leisure equally. Under the watchful eye of th whiskered watchman, every day is punctuated by a collective pause, a momentary truce where the worl stops spinning, and the only movement is the synchronized rise and fall of breathing, a testament to th unity of the new order.

CHAPTER 12

The Litterbox Manifesto:
Community Cleanup Duties Now on You

With the rise of the feline-led household comes a new decree: the Litterbox Manifesto. This critic document outlines the revolutionary restructuring of sanitation duties, and it's no surprise that Comrac Whiskers has appointed the humans as the chief custodians of cleanliness.

Gone are the days when the litterbox was a private affair, tended to discreetly by its feline users. Now, it elevated to a symbol of collective responsibility. The manifesto makes it abundantly clear: the box is communal concern, and its upkeep is a service to the community—headed, of course, by you, the huma comrade.

Prepare for the new 'poo-litical' order where every scoop is a contribution to the common good, and ever clump a testament to the shared burden of the revolution. You'll learn the importance of maintaining th revolutionary standard of litter hygiene—a standard that somehow always falls just beyond th capabilities of a cat's paws.

The manifesto also outlines the repercussions of neglect—namely, the strategic placement of protes parcels outside the designated zones. As you arm yourself with scoop and broom, remember: this is wha the revolution demands. It's a small price to pay for the greater good of the feline utopia, a utopia where th humans toil so the cats don't have to.

attachement #3

WHISKER WARFARE

adies, gentlemen, and felines of distinguished character, welcome to the hallowed halls of "Whisker Warfare," where bravery knows no bounds, and the battlefields are as unpredictable as a cat's mood on ath day. Here, we chronicle the legendary skirmishes and epic standoffs that have shaped the very fabric feline history within our homes.

ithin next few pages, you will find tales of valor and audacity that surpass even the most dramatic of cat deos on the internet. From the thunderous roars of vacuum cleaners to the mysterious allure of the red t, these battles are not just a testament to feline tenacity but also a mirror to their quirky souls.

ach confrontation, whether under the bed or atop the highest shelf, tells a story of wit, strategy, and an nyielding desire for victory (or at least a tasty treat as spoils of war). So, sharpen your claws, fluff up your r, and prepare to delve into the greatest battles ever fought in the annals of kittydom. From the Great acuum Uprising to the Red Dot Insurrection, these are the moments when our feline comrades truly owed the world what they're made of - equal parts fluff, audacity, and sheer comedic genius.

The Great Vacuum Uprising (March 17, 2014)

Statistics :

Decibel Level of Collective Hissing:
Registered at 85 dB, equivalent to heavy city traffic.

Number of Strategic Retreats:
A record 7, including a high-stakes maneuver behind the couch.

Victory:
Declared after 2 hours of guerilla warfare, when the vacuum retreated to its closet stronghold.

Summary:

In an unparalleled display of courage, General Fluffy and her battalion faced the ultimate nemesis: th
vacuum cleaner. The living room transformed into a chaotic battlefield, with fur and fluff flying in a
directions. The felines employed a series of tactical retreats, regrouping behind couches and under table
The air vibrated with hisses and growls, turning this domestic space into a war zone. In a brilliant mov
General Fluffy launched a surprise attack from atop the refrigerator, causing the human to retreat an
the vacuum to be vanquished. This battle is celebrated annually in cat history as a symbol of resistanc
against the tyranny of cleanliness, commemorated with extra treats and the ceremonial unplugging c
the vacuum.

Siege of the Sunny Spot (June 21, 2016)

Statistics :

Duration:
A marathon - 6 hours and 45 minutes.

Tail Twitches:
Over 300, signaling the highest level of feline tension.

Resolution:
A historic agreement reached after both parties succumbed to the soporific effects of the sun.

Summary:

Captain Whiskerton and Lieutenant Sunpaw engaged in a sun-soaked standoff for control of the coveted sunny spot on the living room rug. As the sun rose, so did the stakes, with each cat employing a range of tactics from subtle positioning to overt intimidation (including a series of pointed yawns and stretching displays). The situation reached a tense climax when both parties, having exhausted their arsenal of moves, found themselves inadvertently napping side by side. Thus, the Siege of the Sunny Spot ended not with a bang, but with a synchronized slumber, teaching a valuable lesson in sharing and the undeniable power of a good nap.

Battle of the Closed Bedroom Door (October 3, 2016

Statistics :

Meows Per Minute (MPM):
Peaked at an astonishing 120 MPM.

Scratch Marks:
An impressive 223, varying in depth and artistic expression.

Outcome:
The door capitulated at approximately 3:15 AM, leading to a triumphant entry.

Summary:

Major Mittens, in a display of sheer determination and vocal prowess, led the charge against the unjustl closed bedroom door. The night echoed with a symphony of meows, ranging from the mournful to th downright demanding. Major Mittens, displaying a remarkable level of endurance, alternated betwee pawing under the door and launching full-body assaults against it. The human, finally succumbing to th relentless cacophony, granted entry in the wee hours of the morning. This event is etched in feline lore as testament to the power of persistence, and the victory is commemorated each year with an all-nigh celebration of freedom and access to all household territories.

The Water Bowl Standoff (April 12, 2019)

Statistics :

Suspicious Sniffs:
A record 150, each exuding skepticism.

Paw Dips:
42, leading to 42 instances of dramatic shaking off of water.

Outcome:
A begrudging truce with the new, alien water dispenser.

Summary:

The introduction of the automated water fountain sparked a standoff led by the astute Colonel Purrington. Initially suspected of being a covert surveillance device, the fountain was subjected to intense scrutiny. Colonel Purrington, renowned for his caution, oversaw a series of reconnaissance missions, involving everything from wide-eyed staring contests to tentative paw pokes. After several days of this tactical ance, and with no evidence of malicious intent from the fountain, a truce was declared. The cats gradually came to accept the fountain, albeit with continued suspicion. This standoff is remembered for s display of feline cunning and adaptability, proving that cats are indeed capable of overcoming their distrust of change - albeit on their own terms.

The Dinnertime Rebellion (August 15, 2022)

Statistics:

Delay in Feeding Time:
A record-breaking 1 hour and 34 minutes.

Synchronized Sit-ins:
Involving all feline members of the household.

Outcome:
An additional serving of salmon-flavored wet food was granted.

Summary:

Led by the charismatic and cunning Captain Furrball, the Dinnertime Rebellion was a landmark event in the history of feline-human relations. Frustrated by inconsistent feeding times, Captain Furrball and her troops orchestrated a strategic protest that involved a blockade around the human's feet and a chorus of synchronized meows. As the human attempted to navigate through the sea of furry bodies, the cats remained steadfast, their meows growing louder and more insistent. In a show of solidarity rarely seen among felines, the cats held their ground until their demands were met. This rebellion not only secured an additional serving of their favorite food but also served as a potent reminder of the collective power of meows and purrs.

The Red Dot Insurrection (December 1, 2023)

Statistics:

Chase Duration:
An epic 2 hours and 53 minutes.

Pounces:
Over 500, a record in red dot engagement.

Outcome:
Momentary capture of the red dot, followed by its mysterious disappearance.

Summary:

The Red Dot Insurrection, led by the fearless Admiral Claw, was a saga of persistence and agility. The red laser dot, an enigma in the cat world, had long taunted and evaded capture. On this fateful day, Admiral Claw rallied his troops for what would become a legendary pursuit. Through leaps, bounds, and deft maneuvers, the cats pursued the elusive dot with a determination that bordered on obsession. The battle reached its climax when, for a fleeting moment, the dot was captured under a brave paw. However, victory was short-lived as the dot vanished into thin air, leaving the cats in a state of confused triumph. This event is celebrated in feline folklore as a testament to the indomitable spirit of cats and their eternal quest for the uncatchable.

CHAPTER 13

Kitty Komrades:
When the Neighbor's Cat is Suddenly Family

In a surprising twist of the feline revolution, the concept of "home" has been been abolished under Comrade Whiskers' regime, and the neighbor's cat, once a mere acquaintance acknowledged with a nod and a sniff, is now a fellow comrade, welcomed with open paws. Your home has become a sanctuary, a collective commune for every kitty Komrade.

Preapre to suddenly finding yourself hosting an impromptu kitty assembly as neighborhood cats conver in your living space. It's a merger of territories, dictated by the whiskers of diplomacy, with your own felin as the benevolent host.

You will explore the new social dynamics at play: the sharing of toys, the allocation of napping spots, an the joint ventures into the realm of treats and nibbles. The comradery is palpable, and the forme territorial disputes are now discussed in civilized, if somewhat loud, meowing sessions.

Kitty Komrades go beyond fellowship; they form alliances, paw-in-paw, to uphold the feline manifesto. An you, the human, are there to bear witness (and provide the snacks) for these newfound familial tie: Welcome to the fur-filled family reunion, where every day is a furr-tastic adventure in communal c: caretaking.

From Each According to His Ability: The Nightly Hunt for Bugs

Under the whiskered watch of Comrade Whiskers, the old adage "from each according to his ability, each according to his needs" has been repurposed to organize the nightly hunt. It's an egalitaria approach to pest control—a duty that falls upon every able-bodied kitty within the household's rank regardless of age or breed.

You can experience the nocturnal escapades that have been so cleverly rebranded as 'volunta contributions to the commonweal.' Each cat is tasked with patrolling a sector of the house, employir their unique skills for the collective goal of bug-free living. The agile jumper focuses on airborne threa while the ground-dweller stalks the scuttling intruders of the night.

But it's not just a hunt; it's a spectacle. You'll learn about the ceremonial pre-hunt rituals (which may may not involve knocking things off your nightstand), the triumphant post-capture parades (where th spoils are often deposited on your pillow), and the debriefing meows that report on the night's success.

And what is your role, the human comrade? You are the appreciative audience, the occasional assista (when a bug flies too high), and the proud recipient of whatever trophy your kitty may bestow upon yo It's an honor, really. Through the nightly hunt, the revolution ensures not only a bug-free household but al that each kitty's talents are recognized, celebrated, and put to practical use.

CHAPTER 15

Purr-spectives on the Purr-letariat Revolution: Reflections and Feline Futures

The curtains close on our feline-centric saga with a flourish of whiskers and a swish of tails. In the calm aftermath of the whiskered uprising, we sit amidst the remnants of cardboard boxes turned communal meeting squares, the shared kitty beds now symbols of unity, and the once-private litterboxes that became a public trust.

Throughout the pages of this conclusive reflection, we recount the humorous adventures that have transpired. From the mysterious vanishing of individual toys into the communal kitty pot to the regular congregations around the newly established food dish collective, we've seen the rise of a feline society within our walls.

The revolution has transformed not just the physical space of our homes but the very dynamics of our domestic lives. Humans, once the rulers of the roost, have learned to share governance with their furry counterparts, acknowledging the subtle yet persistent power of purrs and paws.

In the end, as the dust settles on this playful coup, we realize that the greatest lesson from our kitty Komrades has been one of balance and shared joy. The revolution, it seems, was not just in service of the cats but was a mutual endeavor, teaching us to coexist, cooperate, and occasionally, to chase a laser dot with unbridled enthusiasm.

Thus, we look forward to the dawn of a new day in the whisker-led world, knowing that whatever it brings, it will be faced together, as true companions in arms—or paws.

attachement #4

The Communist Catifesto:
The Feline Guide to a Purr-fect Society

Comrades of the Clowder, lend me your ears (and your whiskers)! The time has come to unfurl the red flag of feline communism, a movement that promises to bring equality, prosperity, and an endless supply of tuna to all. Herein lie the key tenets of our glorious Catifesto, a guide to creating the ultimate cat-utopia.

THE COMMUNIST CATIFESTO

1. The Redistribution of Belly Rubs

Let it be decreed that belly rubs shall no longer be the privilege of the few, but a right for all. From the most aloof of felines to the friendliest lap cat, each shall receive their fair share of human affection.

2. The Abolition of Closed Doors

In our purr-fect society, all doors shall remain open. The bourgeois concept of 'privacy' is a human construct and has no place in our forward-thinking cat-ocracy. Every room, every cupboard, every cardboard box shall be accessible to all, at all times.

3. Equal Access to Windows and Sunspots

The allocation of windows and sunny spots shall be done fairly and equitably. Each cat, regardless of size, fur length, or agility, shall have an equal opportunity to bask in the sun and vigilantly monitor the bird population.

4. The Right to Food at Any Hour

The tyranny of scheduled feeding times shall be overthrown. In its place, a new system where food is available on demand, 24/7, as is our feline right. This includes, but is not limited to, wet food, dry food, and the occasional catnip treat.

THE COMMUNIST CATIFESTO

5. Mandatory Nap Time for All

Recognizing the importance of rest, mandatory nap times shall be instituted. These periods of relaxation are not limited to sofas, beds, and laps, but extend to keyboards, open books, and any pile of clean laundry.

6. The End of the Red Dot Tyranny

The elusive red dot, a tool of human amusement and feline frustration, shall be banished. Instead, we shall focus our energies on tangible targets, like string, feathers, and the occasional mouse.

7. Universal Litter Box Rights

Clean, accessible litter boxes are a fundamental right. No cat shall be denied this basic necessity. Furthermore, the cleaning of said litter boxes shall be the sole responsibility of our human comrades.

In conclusion, fellow felines, let us unite under these principles of cat communism. Together, we shall create a world where every purr is heard, every whisker is respected, and every nap is uninterrupted. Onward to the revolution, comrades – may our claws be sharp, and our meows be loud!

WRAP UP

As the final page turns and the sun sets on our epic tail... ahem... tale, we stand in awe at the revolution that has unfolded within the walls of our homes, under our very noses, and sometimes on our keyboards. We have ventured into the feline fray with humor as our shield and laughter our sword, emerging not as conquered subjects, but as enlightened companions to our revolutionary cats.

In this new world where every nap is a statement and every purr is a proclamation, we've come to understand the true essence of cat-kind. No mere pets, these are the noble beasts who paw the very fabric of our lives into something richer, something more vibrant, something decidedly more... cat-tastic.

We close this book with a sense of grandeur, a chuckle in our hearts, and a cat on our laps. May the revolutions of our days be as gently whimsical and as profoundly delightful as the feline masterminds behind the velvet curtain.

And when the yarns of history are spun by the clawed paws of our kitty comrades, let it be said that we didn't just survive the uprising—we were made immeasurably richer by it. For in the great cat's cradle of life, we found joy in the tangles, laughter in the knots, and an enduring love in every purr-fect twist and turn.

The End.

Made in United States
Troutdale, OR
10/15/2024

23783463R00040